CAMBRIDGE ENGLISH QUALIFICATIONS

Practice Tests Pre A1 Starters

• PETRINA CLIFF •

Four practice tests

OXFORD
UNIVERSITY PRESS

OXFORD
UNIVERSITY PRESS

Great Clarendon Street, Oxford, OX2 6DP, United Kingdom

Oxford University Press is a department of the University of Oxford.
It furthers the University's objective of excellence in research, scholarship,
and education by publishing worldwide. Oxford is a registered trade
mark of Oxford University Press in the UK and in certain other countries

ISBN: 978 0 19 404258 1 — Cambridge English Qualifications Pre A1 Starters Practice Tests Pack

ISBN: 978 0 19 404259 8 — Cambridge English Qualifications Pre A1 Starters Practice Tests Student Book

ISBN: 978 0 19 404261 1 — Cambridge English Qualifications Pre A1 Starters Practice Tests Audio access card

ISBN: 978 0 19 404260 4 — Cambridge English Qualifications Practice Tests Audio

Printed in China

This book is printed on paper from certified and well-managed sources

ACKNOWLEDGEMENTS

Back cover photograph: Oxford University Press building/David Fisher

Illustrations by:

Cover by Peter Stevenson/Linden Artists

Peter Stevenson Linden Artists pp.title page, 5, 7–13, 15–20, 33–41, 43–47, 52

Jon Davis with colouring by Steven Jenkinsons pp.21–23, 26, 29–31, 49–51, 54, 55, 57–67

Judy Brown pp.4, 10, 14, 18, 23, 28, 32, 42, 46

Gary Parsons pp.11, 13, 14, 24, 25, 27, 42, 52, 56

Contents

Part 1

- 5 questions -

Listen and draw lines. There is one example.

Dan   May   Eva   Lucy

Matt   Anna   Sam

Part 2

- 5 questions -

Read the question. Listen and write a name or a number.

There are two examples.

Examples

What is Alice's brother's name?   ....Tom..........

How old is he?   ....5...........

Questions

1   What is Alice's sister's name?   ....

2   How many people are there in Alice's family?   ....

3   How many rooms are there in Alice's house?   ....

4   How many posters are there in Alice's bedroom?   ....

5   What's the name of Alice's favourite toy?   ....

Part 3

- 5 questions -

Listen and tick (✔) the box. There is one example.

Which is Kim?

A   **B** ☐   **C** ☐

1   What's Bill doing?

A ☐   **B** ☐   **C** ☐

2   Which is Mrs. White?

A ☐   **B** ☐   **C** ☐

3   What's Pat doing today?

A ☐

B ☐

C ☐

4   What are Ben and Tom doing?

A ☐

B ☐

C ☐

5   What's Nick's hobby?

A ☐

B ☐

C ☐

Part 4

- 5 questions -

Listen and colour. There is one example.

Reading & Writing

Part 1
- 5 questions -

Look and read. Put a tick (✔) or a cross (✗) in the box. There are two examples.

Examples

This is a lorry.

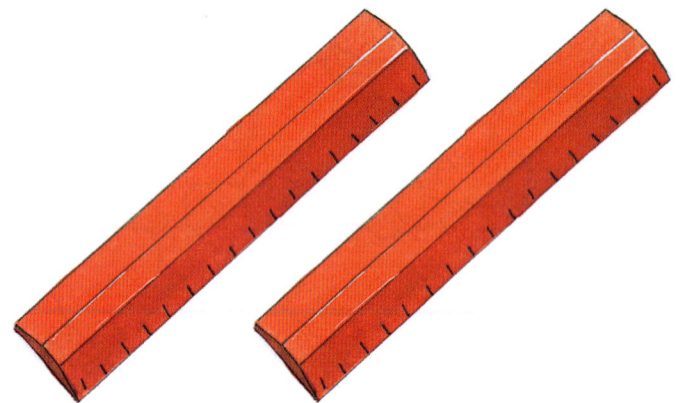

These are crayons.

Questions

1

This is a bee.

2

These are bears. □

3

This is a guitar. □

4

This is a rug. □

5

These are lemons. □

Part 2

- 5 questions -

Look and read. Write yes or no. There are two examples.

Examples

The monster has got 2 heads. ....yes..........

The woman is wearing a pink skirt. ....no..........

Questions

1   The cat is in front of the tree. ....

2   A boy is riding a horse. ....

3   Two children are talking. ....

4   There is a mouse in the bag. ....

5   There are three spiders next to the house. ....

Part 3

- 5 questions -

Look at the pictures. Look at the letters. Write the words. There is one example.

Example

m i r r o r

r
i   m   r
r   o

Questions

1

_ _ _ _

m
p   a   l

2

_ _ _ _ _

d   o
r
i
a

3

_ _ _ _ _ _

d   i
w   n   w
o

4

_ _ _ _ _ _ _ _

c   o   s
b   a   k   e
o

5

_ _ _ _ _ _ _ _

i   a
t   g   n   i
p   n

Part 4

- 5 questions -

Read this. Choose a word from the box. Write the correct word next to numbers 1-5. There is one example.

Chocolate

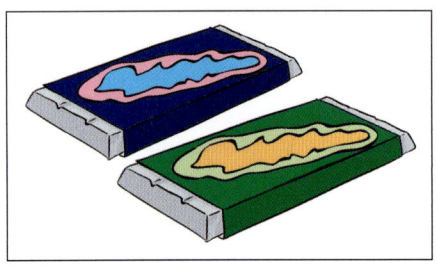

People go to a ......shop...... and buy chocolate there. Really nice

chocolates come in **(1)** .... For your friend's birthday you can

get a nice present, like a book or a **(2)** .... Then go in the

kitchen and make a chocolate **(3)** .... too. And on a hot day it's

really good to sit on the **(4)** .... and have a chocolate ice cream.

(5) .... love chocolate and mums and dads do too!

Part 5

- 5 questions -

**Look at the pictures and read the questions. Write one-word answers.
There are two examples.**

Examples

How many people are there in the car? ....3...........

What are the boys doing? eating ....chips.........

Questions

1 Which animal is in front of the car? ....

2   Where is the family now?   on the ....

3   What are Mum and Dad doing?   ....

4   What game are the girl and dog playing?   ....

5   What is the chicken doing now?   bouncing a ....

Speaking

Part 1
- 5 questions -

Listen and draw lines. There is one example.

Alice   Hugo   Jill   Pat

Sam   Grace   Tom

Part 2

- 5 questions -

Read the question. Listen and write a name or a number.

There are two examples.

Examples

What's the boy's name?   ....Tom.........

How old is he?   ....7............

Questions

1 What's the name of Tom's pet mouse?   ....

2 How old is Tom's pet mouse?   ....

3 What is Tom's mum's name?   ....

4 How many brothers and sisters does Tom have?   ....

5 What is Tom's Grandma's name?   ....

Part 3

- 5 questions -

Listen and tick (✔) the box. There is one example.

Where's the handbag?

A ☐   B ✔   C ☐

1   What are Mark and Eva doing?

A ☐   B ☐   C ☐

2   Which is Nick's picture?

A ☐   B ☐   C ☐

3   Where does Anna live?

A ☐   B ☐   C ☐

4   How does Alex go to school?

A ☐   B ☐   C ☐

5   What does Bill eat for breakfast?

A ☐   B ☐   C ☐

Part 4

- 5 questions -

Listen and colour. There is one example.

Reading & Writing

Part 1
- 5 questions -

Look and read. Put a tick (✔) or a cross (✗) in the box. There are two examples.

Examples

These are meatballs.

This is a tablet.

Questions

1

This is a baseball cap.

2

This is a teddy bear. ☐

3

These are trains. ☐

4

This is a shirt. ☐

5

These are boots. ☐

Part 2

Look and read. Write yes or no. There are two examples.

Examples

The car is red. ....yes..........

There is a jellyfish in the water. ....no..........

Questions

1   The tiger is between the giraffe and the goat. ....

2   There are two people in the car. ....

3   There is a lizard under the tree. ....

4   The monkey has got a banana in its hand. ....

5   There is a zebra next to the elephant. ....

Part 3

- 5 questions -

Look at the pictures. Look at the letters. Write the words. There is one example.

Example

a p p l e

e p a
l p

Questions

1

_ _ _ _

e
c   i
r

2

_ _ _ _ _

r
d a e
b

3

_ _ _ _ _ _

o a
e g r
n

4

_ _ _ _

i
w k
i

5

_ _ _

e
i p

27

Part 4

Read this. Choose a word from the box. Write the correct word next to numbers 1-5. There is one example.

Painting

Lots of people enjoy painting in a ......park...... . They paint pictures

of the flowers and (**1**) .... there. Or they go to the beach to

do paintings of the boats and (**2**) .... in the sea. You can take

photos of these things with a (**3**) .... but paintings can be really

cool. Painting at (**4**) .... with your classmates is good fun too.

Then you can put your favourite (**5**) .... on your bedroom wall.

It's a great hobby. Do you like painting?

example

park   ships   school   duck

trees   kitchen   painting   camera

Part 5

- 5 questions -

**Look at the pictures and read the questions. Write one-word answers.
There are two examples.**

Examples

What is the girl doing?   riding a   ....bike..........

How many kites has the boy got?   ....two..........

Questions

1   What is the boy's father doing?   ....

2   What is the boy's father holding?   ....

3   How many spiders are there?   ....

4   What are the boy and his father doing now?   ....

5   Where is the girl sitting?   on the ....

Speaking

Part 1

- 5 questions -

Listen and draw lines. There is one example.

Bill   Lucy   Matt   Grace

Pat   Dan   May

Part 2

Read the question. Listen and write a name or a number.

There are two examples.

Examples

What's Anna's friend's name?   ....Lucy.........

How old is she?   ....9...........

Questions

1 How many children go to school on the bus?   ....

2 How many children are there in Anna's class?   ....

3 What is Anna's teacher's name?   ....

4 How many lessons does Anna have in the morning? ....

5 What is Anna's cat's name?   ....

Part 3

- 5 questions -

Listen and tick (✔) the box. There is one example.

What does Ben want for his birthday?

 A ☐

 B ✔

 C ☐

1 Where's the bread?

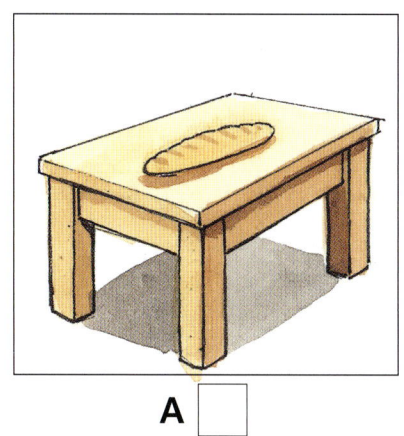 A ☐

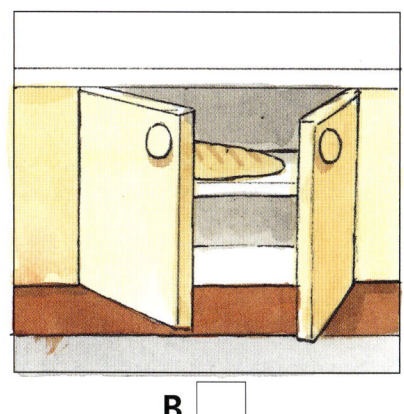 B ☐

 C ☐

2 Who's got the school book?

 A ☐

 B ☐

 C ☐

3   What's Nick doing?

A

B

C

4   Which girl is Alex's sister?

A

B

C

5   What's Kim's favourite animal?

A

B

C

Part 4

- 5 questions -

Listen and colour. There is one example.

Reading & Writing

Part 1

- 5 questions -

Look and read. Put a tick (✔) or a cross (✗) in the box. There are two examples.

Examples

This is a coconut.   ✔

This is a poster.   ✗

Questions

1

These are tennis rackets.   ☐

2

This is a potato. ☐

3

These are jellyfish. ☐

4

This is a window. ☐

5

This is a dining room. ☐

Part 2

- 5 questions -

Look and read. Write yes or no. There are two examples.

Examples

There is a radio under the table. ....yes..........

The fruit is behind the boy. ....no..........

Questions

1 It is five o'clock. ....

2 There is a photo between the flowers and the goat. ....

3 The man is sitting in an armchair. ....

4 The window is open. ....

5 The robot is on the rug. ....

Part 3

- 5 questions -

Look at the pictures. Look at the letters. Write the words. There is one example.

Example

b u s

u s b

Questions

1

_ _ _ _

h
p   i
s

2

_ _ _ _ _

l
n   a   p
e

3

_ _ _ _ _

y
r   l   o
r

4

_ _ _ _ _

r   i
a   n
t

5

_ _ _ _ _ _ _ _ _

o   i
t   o   e   m
k   r   b

Part 4

- 5 questions -

Read this. Choose a word from the box. Write the correct word next to numbers 1-5. There is one example.

Your bedroom

In your bedroom you can you can lie on the ....bed....... and listen to

your favourite music. Then you can sit at your **(1)** .... and work,

or write and draw pictures with pencils and **(2)** .... Children put

(3) .... on their bedroom walls. On these you can see the people

and things they really like. There's a **(4)** .... in your bedroom for

all your clothes and **(5)** .... And at night you go to bed in your

bedroom and then you go to sleep.

Part 5

- 5 questions -

Look at the pictures and read the questions. Write one-word answers.
There are two examples.

Examples

What are the children doing? playing with a ....ball..........

Where is the woman?   under a ....tree..........

Questions

1   How many birds are there in the picture?   ....

2   What is the woman doing?   ....

3   Where is the ball?   in her ....

4   Who has got the ball now?   the ....

5   What is the woman doing now?   ....

Speaking

Part 1

- 5 questions -

Listen and draw lines. There is one example.

Bill   Alice   Nick   Kim

Hugo   Eva   Alex

Part 2

- 5 questions -

Read the question. Listen and write a name or a number.

There are two examples.

Examples

How old is Ben?   ....7...........

What is Ben's Grandpa's name?   ....Sam.........

Questions

1   What is Ben's Grandma's name?   ....

2   How many cows has Ben's Grandpa got?   ....

3   What's the horse's name?   ....

4   How old is the horse?   ....

5   How many baby sheep are there?   ....

Part 3
- 5 questions -

Listen and tick (✔) the box. There is one example.

Which is Sam's bedroom?

A ☐   B ✔   C ☐

1   What's Sue drawing?

A ☐   B ☐   C ☐

2   Which is Anna's house?

A ☐   B ☐   C ☐

3   What's Ben's Mum doing today?

A   B   C

4   What does Bill want to eat?

A   B   C

5   Where's Tom's Dad?

A   B   C

Part 4

- 5 questions -

Listen and colour. There is one example.

Reading & Writing

Part 1

- 5 questions -

Look and read. Put a tick (✔) or a cross (✘) in the box. There are two examples.

Examples

This is a lizard.

This is a beach.

Questions

1

This is a polar bear.

2

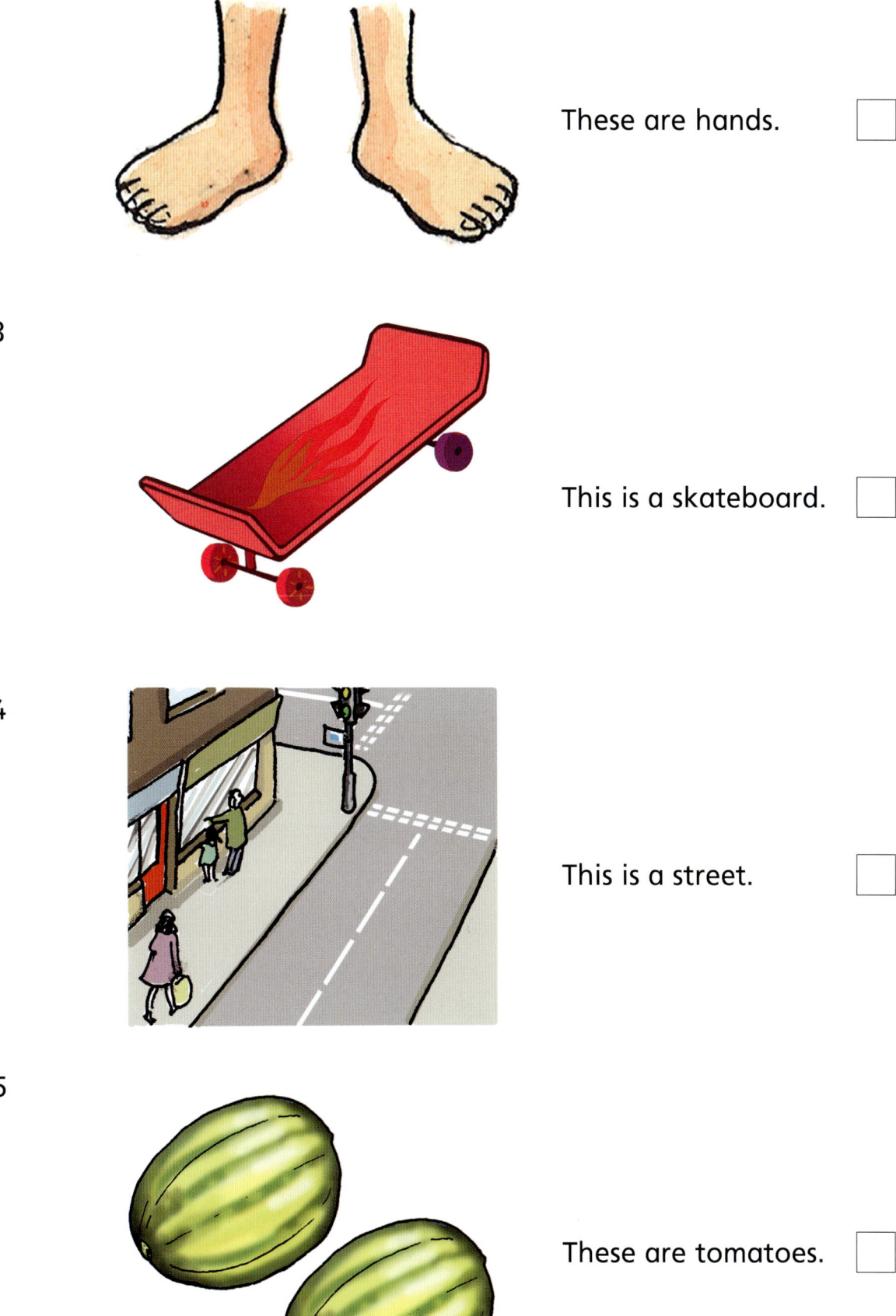

These are hands. ☐

3

This is a skateboard. ☐

4

This is a street. ☐

5

These are tomatoes. ☐

Part 2

- 5 questions -

Look and read. Write yes or no. There are two examples.

Examples

The woman is walking with her dog. ....yes..........

There's a bike under the chair. ....no..........

Questions

1 The man is eating. ....

2 There are four ice creams in the picture. ....

3 The children are in front of the shop. ....

4 The girl in the boat is waving. ....

5 There is a hat in the water
   between two lizards. ....

Part 3

- 5 questions -

Look at the pictures. Look at the letters. Write the words. There is one example.

Example

s o c k

c s k o

Que:

1

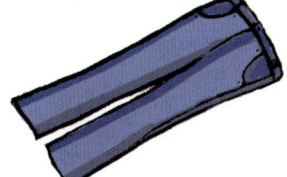

— — — — —

e n
j   a
s

2

— — — — —

s
r   s   d
e

3

— — — — —

h   r
t   s   s
o

4

— — — — — —

k   a
t   c   e
j

5

— — — — — — —

s   g
l   e   a
s   s

Part 4

- 5 questions -

Read this. Choose a word from the box. Write the correct word next to numbers 1-5. There is one example.

Polar bears

A lot of bears are brown, but polar bears have a white body and a

beautiful face, with a black nose and two small brown eyes. With their

big **(1)** .... they can run very fast. They don't like the hot

(2) .... but love swimming in a really cold **(3)** ....

They enjoy catching and eating **(4)** .... , but they eat meat too.

You can see polar bears at the **(5)** .... They can be scary, but

they're fantastic animals!

Part 5

- 5 questions -

Look at the pictures and read the questions. Write one-word answers. There are two examples.

Examples

How many frogs are there? ....two..........

What is the teacher doing?   drawing a   ......pineapple......

Questions

1   What colour are the fish?   ....

2   Who is pointing to the frogs?   ....

3   Where are the frogs now?   under the ....

4   What is the teacher holding?   a ....

5   Where are the children putting the frogs?   in the ....

Speaking

Test 1 Speaking

Test 3   Speaking

Starters Vocabulary List

n = noun
num = number
pron = pronoun
inter = interjection

v = verb
det = determiner
int = interrogative
excl = exclamation

adj = adjective
adv = adverb
dis = discourse marker

prep = preposition
conj = conjunction

A

a **det**
about **prep**
add **v**
afternoon **n**
again **adv**
Alice **n**
alphabet **n**
am **v**
an **det**
and **conj**
animal **n**
answer **n + v**
apple **n**
are **v**
arm **n**
armchair **n**
ask **v**
at **prep**

B

baby **n**
badminton **n**
bag **n**
ball **n**
banana **n**
baseball **n**
baseball cap **n**
basketball **n**
bath **n**
bathroom **n**
be **v**
beach **n**
bean **n**
bear **n**
beautiful **adj**
bed **n**
bedroom **n**
bee **n**
behind **prep**

Ben **n**
between **prep**
big **adj**
bike **n**
Bill **n**
bird **n**
birthday **n**
black **adj**
blue **adj**
board **n**
board game **n**
boat **n**
body **n**
book **n**
bookcase **n**
boots **n**
bounce **v**
box **n**
boy **n**
bread **n**
breakfast **n**
brother **n**
brown **adj**
burger **n**
bus **n**
but **conj**
bye

C

cake **n**
camera **n**
can/cannot/can't **v**
car **n**
carrot **n**
cat **n**
catch **v**
chair **n**
chicken **n**
child/children **n**
chips **n**

choose **v**
clap **v**
class **n**
classmates **n**
classroom **n**
clean **adj + v**
clock **n**
close **v**
clothes **n**
coconut **n**
colour **n**
colour (in) **v**
come **v**
complete **v**
computer **n**
cool **adj + excl**
correct **adj**
cousin **n**
cow **n**
crayons **n**
crocodile **n**
cross **n + v**
cupboard **n**

D

dad **n**
day **n**
desk **n**
dining room **n**
dirty **adj**
do/don't **v**
dog **n**
doll **n**
donkey **n**
door **n**
double **adj**
draw **v**
drawing **n**
dress **n**
drink **n + v**

drive **v**
duck **n**

E

ear **n**
eat **v**
egg **n**
eight **num**
elephant **n**
end **n**
English **n** + **adj**
enjoy **v**
eraser **n**
evening **n**
example **n**
Eva **n**
eye **n**

F

face **n**
family **n**
fantastic **adj** + **excl**
father **n**
favourite **adj** + **n**
find **v**
fish (s + pl) **n**
fishing **n**
five **num**
flat **n**
floor **n**
floor **n**
flower **n**
fly **v**
food **n**
foot/feet **n**
football **n**
for **prep**
four **num**
French fries **n**
friend **n**
frog **n**
from **prep**
fruit **n**
fun **n**
funny **adj**

G

game **n**

garden **n**
get **v**
giraffe **n**
girl **n**
give **v**
glasses **n**
go **v**
goat **n**
good **adj**
good-bye
got **v**
go to bed **v**
go to sleep **v**
grandfather **n**
grandma **n**
grandmother **n**
grandpa **n**
great **adj**
green **adj**
grey (or gray) **adj**
guitar **n**

H

hair **n**
hall **n**
hand **n**
handbag **n**
happy **adj**
(Happy birthday)
hat **n**
have (got) **v**
have (a bath, a drink,
food) **v**
he **pron**
head **n**
helicopter **n**
hello
her **pron**
here **adv**
hers **pron**
hi **excl**
him **pron**
hippo **n**
his **pron**
hit **v**
hobby **n**
hockey **n**
hold **v**
hooray **excl**

horse **n**
house **n**
how **int** (How do you
spell it?)
how many **int**
how old **int**
Hugo **n**

I

I **pron**
in **prep**
in front of **prep**
is **v**
it **pron**
its **pron**

J

jacket **n**
jeans **n**
jellyfish **n**
juice **n**
jump **v**

K

kick **v**
kids **n**
Kim **n**
kitchen **n**
kite **n**
kiwi **n**
know (don't know) **v**

L

lamp **n**
learn **v**
leg **n**
lemon **n**
lemonade **n**
lesson **n**
let's **v**
letter (as in alphabet) **n**
like **v** + **prep**
lime **n**
line **n**
listen (to) **v**
live **v**
living room **n**

lizard n
long adj
look v
look at v
lorry n
a lot adv + pron
lots adv + pron
a lot of det
lots of det
love v
lunch n

M

make v
man/men n
mango n
many det
Mark n
mat n
Matt n
May (girl's name) n
me pron
meat n
meatballs n
milk n
mine pron
mirror n
Miss (title)
monkey n
monster n
mother n
motorbike n
mouse/mice n
mouth n
Mr (title)
Mrs (title)
mum n
my det

N

name n
new adj
next to prep
nice adj
Nick n
night n
nine num
no det
nose n

not adv
now adv + dis
number n

O

of prep
oh inter + dis
OK inter + dis
old adj
on prep
one num
onion n
open v
or conj
orange n + adj
our adj
ours adj

P

page n
paint n + v
painting n
pardon inter
park n
part n
Pat n
pea n
pear n
pen n
pencil n
person / people n
pet n
phone n + v
photo n
piano n
pick up v
picture n
pie n
pineapple n
pink adj
plane n
play with v
please inter
point v
point to v
polar bear n
poster n
potato n
purple adj

put v

Q

question n

R

radio n
read v
red adj
rice n
ride n + v
right (correct) adj + dis
robot n
room n
rubber n
rug n
ruler n
run n

S

sad adj
Sam n
sand n
sausage n
say v
scary adj
school n
sea n
see v
sentence n
seven num
she pron
sheep (s + pl) n
shell n
ship n
shirt n
shoe n
shop n
short adj
shorts n
show v
silly adj
sing v
sister n
sit (down) v
six num
skateboard n
skirt n

sleep **v**
small **adj**
snake **n**
so **dis**
soccer **n**
sock **n**
sofa **n**
some **det**
song **n**
sorry **inter + adj**
spell **v**
spider **n**
sport **n**
stand (up) **v**
start **v**
stop **v**
story **n**
street **n**
Sue **n**
sun **n**
swim **v**

T

T shirt **n**
table **n**
tablet **n**
table tennis **n**
take (a photo) **v**
talk **v**
teacher **n**
teddy bear **n**
television/TV **n**
tell **v**
ten **num**
tennis **n**
tennis racket **n**
thank you
that **det + pron**
the **det**
their **det**
theirs **det**
them **pron**
then **dis**
there **dummy subject**
there **adv**
these **det + pron**
they **pron**
thing **n**
this **det + pron**

those **det + pron**
three **num**
throw **v**
tick **n + v**
tiger **n**
to **prep**
today **n + adv**
Tom **n**
tomato **n**
too **adv**
toy **n**
train **n**
tree **n**
trousers **n**
truck **n**
try **v**
two **num**

U

ugly **adj**
under **prep**
understand **v**
us **pron**

V

very **adv**

W

walk **v**
wall **n**
want **v**
watch **n + v**
water **n**
watermelon **n**
wave **v**
we **pron**
wear **v**
well **dis**
what **int**
where **int**
which **int**
white **adv**
who **int**
whose **int**
window **n**
with **prep**
woman/women **n**
word **n**

write **v**

X

(no words at this level)

Y

yellow **adj**
yes
you **pron**
young **adj**
your **pron + adj**

Z

zebra **n**
zoo **n**